THE SCOTLAND
COLOURING BOOK

First published 2016
Reprinted 2017, 2019

The History Press
97 St George's Place,
Cheltenham, GL50 3QB
www.thehistorypress.co.uk

British Library Cataloguing in Publication Data.
A catalogue record for this book is available from the British Library.

ISBN 978 0 7509 6781 5

Cover colouring by Lucy Hester.
Typesetting and origination by The History Press
Printed in Turkey by Imak.

THE SCOTLAND
COLOURING BOOK

PAST AND PRESENT

Take some time out of your busy life to relax and unwind with this feel-good colouring book designed for everyone who loves Scotland.

Absorb yourself in the simple action of colouring in the scenes and settings from around Scotland, past and present. From iconic cityscapes to picturesque countryside, you are sure to find some of your favourite locations waiting to be transformed with a splash of colour. Bring these scenes alive as you de-stress with this inspiring and calming colouring book.

There are no rules – choose any page and any choice of colouring pens or pencils you like to create your own unique, colourful and creative illustrations.

Arthur's Seat is the main peak of a group of hills in
Edinburgh which form most of Holyrood Park ▸

Edinburgh Old Town is the name popularly given
to the oldest part of Scotland's capital city ▸

Edinburgh Castle. The eleventh-century castle houses the
Crown Jewels and National War Museum of Scotland ▸

Glasgow Cathedral stands majestically
in the heart of Scotland's largest city ▶

The Mitchell Library in Glasgow is
one of Europe's largest public libraries ▸

The pink harled Craigievar Castle in
Aberdeenshire was completed in 1626 ▸

King's College Chapel – seen here in 1869 – is a formerly independent university founded in 1495 and now part of the University of Aberdeen ▸

Bullers of Buchan. The collapsed sea cave forms an almost circular chasm some 98ft deep, where the sea rushes in through a natural archway ▶

The ruins of Slains Castle in Aberdeenshire
overlook the North Sea from its cliff-top site ▶

Fireworks light up the sky during
Hogmanay celebrations in Edinburgh ▶

Built in 1836 by architect William Burn, the red sandstone
Inverness Castle overlooks the River Ness in Inverness ▸

The McManus, Dundee's
Art Gallery and Museum ▸

The ruins of the twelfth-century
St Andrews Cathedral, Fife ▸

The High Kirk of Edinburgh, commonly called
St Giles' Cathedral, is the principal place of worship
of the Church of Scotland in Edinburgh ▸

The ruins of Craigmillar Castle in Edinburgh ▶

Scone Palace, Perth ▸

Culzean Castle. It's easy to see why this
eighteenth-century castle and country park is
one of Scotland's most popular visitor attractions ▸

Branklyn Garden offers visitors 2 acres
of magnificent gardens, set on the side
of Kinnoull Hill overlooking Perth ▸

Oban harbour is a busy working port on the west coast
of Scotland. McCaig's Tower can be seen on the hill ▶

Once one of Scotland's largest castles, Urquhart
Castle on the banks of Loch Ness remains an
impressive stronghold despite its ruinous state ▶

Inveraray Castle has been the seat of the
Duke of Argyll, chief of Clan Campbell,
since the seventeenth century ▶

Deacon Brodie's Tavern,
Lawnmarket, Edinburgh ▸

The ruins of the sixteenth-century Ardvreck
Castle stand on a rocky promontory jutting
out into Loch Assynt in Sutherland ▶

A traditional Scottish bagpiper at Glencoe ▶

Glamis Castle is the home of the Earl and Countess of
Strathmore and Kinghorne, and is open to the public ▸

The Highland Fling is a solo dance that gained
popularity in the early nineteenth century ▸

The snow-covered peak of Ben Nevis.
Standing at 1,344m above sea level,
Ben Nevis is the highest mountain in the UK ▶

Here tugs tow the Ellerman Line's
City of Singapore up the River Clyde in 1951 ▸

Stirling Castle sits atop Castle Hill, Stirling. The castle is a Scheduled Ancient Monument and is now a tourist attraction managed by Historic Scotland ▸

Highland cattle are a Scottish cattle breed. They have long horns and long wavy coats that are coloured black, brindle, red, yellow, white, silver or dun ▶

Glenfinnan Viaduct. Located at the top of Loch Shiel in the West Highlands of Scotland, the viaduct has been used as a location in several films and television series, including the *Harry Potter* film series ▸

Eilean Donan is a small tidal island where three
lochs meet in the western Highlands of Scotland ▶

Newspaper barrow outside the Royal Arch, Dundee docks, pictured here during the Victorian era ▶

Balmoral Castle in Royal Deeside, Aberdeenshire ▸

The Kelvingrove Art Gallery
and Museum, Glasgow ▸

Tobermory is the capital of the Isle of Mull in the
Scottish Inner Hebrides. Many of the buildings
on Main Street are painted in various bright
colours, making it a popular location for television
programmes such as the children's show *Balamory* ▶

The puffin is one of the most
popular seabirds on Orkney ▶

Loch Lomond and the Trossachs National Park ▸

Caledonian Railway No.828 over
Granish Moor near Aviemore ▸

The Old Carr Bridge,
Cairngorms National Park ▸

Shetland ponies on Shetland ▶

Sunset on the Isle of Arran ▶

The National Wallace Monument stands on the summit of Abbey Craig, a hilltop near Stirling. It commemorates the thirteenth-century Scottish hero Sir William Wallace ▸

Edinburgh Zoo is home to the UK's only
giant pandas, Tian Tian and Yang Guang ▸

On 23 and 24 June 1314 Robert the Bruce faced
King Edward II at Bannockburn, near Stirling.
The Scots army was outnumbered almost three
to one but they defeated the English in a pitched
battle that became a significant Scottish victory ▸

Also from The History Press

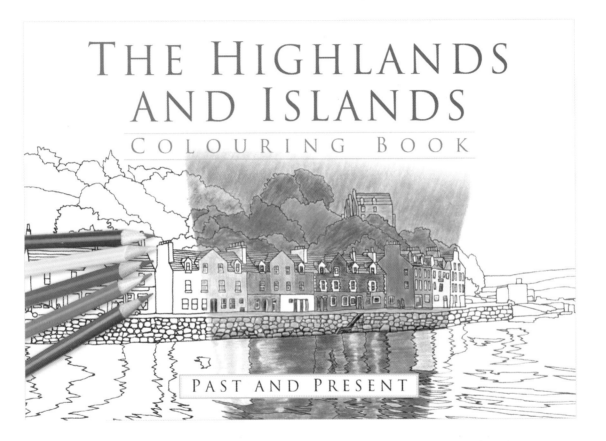

THE HIGHLANDS
AND ISLANDS
COLOURING BOOK

PAST AND PRESENT

Find this colouring book and more at
www.thehistorypress.co.uk